THE
GREAT
PHILOSOPHERS

Consulting Editors
Ray Monk and Frederic Raphael

D1396323

John Cottingham

·····································

DESCARTES

Descartes' Philosophy of Mind

PHŒNIX

A PHOENIX PAPERBACK

First published in Great Britain in 1997 by
Phoenix, a division of the Orion Publishing Group Ltd
Orion House
5 Upper St Martin's Lane
London, WC2H 9EA

Second impression 1998

A CIP catalogue record for this book is available from the British
Library.

ISBN 0 753 80205 8

Typeset by Deltatype Ltd, Birkenhead, Merseyside

Printed in Great Britain by
Clays Ltd, St Ives plc

CONTENTS

ABBREVIATIONS TO SOURCES

AT   C. Adam and P. Tannery (eds), (*Œuvres de Descartes* (12 vols, revised edn, Paris, Vrin/CNRS, 1964–76).

CSM   J. Cottingham, R. Stoothoff and D. Murdoch (eds), *The Philosophical Writings of Descartes*, Vols I and II (Cambridge, Cambridge University Press, 1985).

CSMK   J. Cottingham, R. Stoothoff, D. Murdoch and A. Kenny (eds), *The Philosophical Writings of Descartes*, Vol. III, The Correspondence (Cambridge, Cambridge University Press, 1991).

Note: 'AT' is the standard Franco-Latin edition of the complete works of Descartes. Cross references to 'CSM' and 'CSMK', the standard English edition, are given for the reader's convenience, but in a number of the passages quoted I have made occasional minor alterations in phrasing and/or punctuation. In some of the quotations, I have also put certain key words and phrases in italics to draw the reader's attention to their importance for the argument under discussion.

DESCARTES

Descartes' Philosophy of Mind

ACKNOWLEDGEMENTS

The author and publishers wish to thank the following for permission to use copyright material:

Cambridge University Press for excerpts from *The Philosophical Writings of Descartes*, Vols I & II, eds. J Cottingham, R Stoothoff and D Murdoch (1985); and *The Philosophical Writings of Descartes*, Vol III, eds. J Cottingham, R Stoothoff, D Murdoch and A Kenny (1991);

Every effort has been made to trace the copyright holders but if any have been inadvertently overlooked the publishers will be pleased to make the necessary arrangement at the first opportunity.

1
THE CARTESIAN REVOLUTION

Descartes the scientist

The name of René Descartes is synonymous with the birth of the modern age. The 'new' philosophers, as he and his followers were called in the seventeenth century, inaugurated a fundamental shift in scientific thinking, the effects of which are still with us today. Indeed, Descartes was one of the principal architects of the very notion of 'scientific thinking' as we now understand it. All scientific explanation, Descartes insists, must be expressed in terms of precise, mathematically defined *quantities*:

> I recognize no matter in corporeal things apart from that which the geometers call *quantity*, and take as the object of their demonstrations, i.e. that to which every kind of *division, shape and motion* is applicable. Moreover, my consideration of such matter involves absolutely nothing apart from these divisions, shapes and motions ... And since all natural phenomena can be explained in this way, I do not think that any other principles are either admissible or desirable in physics (*Principles of Philosophy* [1644], Pt II, art. 64).

Our ordinary everyday picture of the world is of course very far from purely quantitative: it involves, apart from size, shape and motion, a host of different qualities – all the various colours, tastes, smells, textures and sounds we are aware of through our five senses. And the traditional 'scholastic' philosophy that had dominated the European universities for many centuries had tended to explain the natural world in terms of just such 'real qualities' ('heaviness', 'moistness', 'dryness', and so on) that were supposed to inhere in things. Today, by contrast, all scientists take it for granted that to try to explain things purely at this 'common sense' level is not enough: we need to probe deeper, to the micro-level, and investigate the interactions between the various particles out of which our ordinary world of medium-sized objects is composed. Descartes' resounding declaration of his scientific principles underlines just this need. Physics, from henceforth, becomes the investigation of explanatory mechanisms operating at the micro-level; and the operations of those mechanisms have to be described in the exact language of mathematics.

But Descartes' vision of science was yet more ambitious. He insisted that the same underlying explanatory schema held good for all observable phenomena, ranging from the vast revolutions of the heavenly bodies down to events in the atmosphere and on the earth's surface, and even the microscopic processes going on inside our own bodies. He was, in short, a *reductionist*; that is, he claimed that all natural phenomena, terrestrial or celestial, organic or inorganic, no matter how striking their surface differences, can be reduced to, or fully explained in terms of, the elementary mechanics of the particles out of which the relevant objects are made up:

Consider how amazing are the properties of magnets

4

and of fire, and how different they are from the properties we commonly observe in other bodies: how a huge and massively powerful flame can be instantaneously kindled from a tiny spark when it falls on a large quantity of powder; or how the stars radiate their light instantly in every direction over such an enormous distance. In this volume I have deduced the causes – which I believe to be quite evident – of these and many other phenomena from principles which are known to all and admitted by all, namely the *shape, size, position and motion of particles of matter*. And anyone who considers all this will readily be convinced that there are no powers in stones and plants that are so mysterious, and no marvels attributed to 'sympathetic' and 'antipathetic' influences that are so astonishing, that they cannot be explained in this way. In short there is nothing in the whole of nature ... which is incapable of being deductively explained on the basis of these self-same principles (*Principles of Philosophy*, Pt IV, art. 187).

All of science becomes, for Descartes, an integrated whole – a great *tree* of knowledge (to use one metaphor he favoured), where the solid trunk of physics branches off into all sorts of particular sciences (like medicine), but without departing from the same fundamental set of explanatory principles (cf. *Principles of Philosophy*, Preface to French edition of 1647).

But there is one exception. In the triumphant exposition of the Cartesian scientific creed just quoted, one crucial phrase has been omitted from the final sentence. What Descartes in fact added was the vital caveat which, in some form or another, he always inserted when extolling the scope and range of his new scientific programme:

> In short there is nothing in the whole of nature, *nothing, that is, which should be referred to purely corporeal causes, i.e. those devoid of thought and mind,* which is incapable of being explained on the basis of these self-same principles.

With the phenomena of 'thought and mind' the grand Cartesian project of explanatory science grinds to a halt. For Descartes divides reality into two fundamental categories: in addition to *res extensa* ('extended substance') – the three-dimensional world of physics, a world explicable entirely in terms of moving particles of a specified size and shape – there is the quite distinct realm of *thought*. Each conscious mind is a *res cogitans* or 'thinking substance', a being whose essential characteristics are entirely independent of matter and wholly *in*explicable via the quantitative language of physics.

Descartes' 'dualistic' division of reality into two fundamentally distinct kinds of entity – thinking stuff and extended stuff – bequeathed a massive conundrum for philosophy that has been with us ever since: what exactly is the nature of consciousness, and what is its relationship to the physical world? Not many modern philosophers are much enamoured with Descartes' own position (that thought is the property of an entirely immaterial substance); but all agree that the 'mind–body problem', as it has come to be known, is a philosophical-cum-scientific puzzle of enormous importance, and that Descartes' ideas on the subject have had, for good or ill, an extraordinarily pervasive influence on subsequent ways of approaching it.

Descartes' famous, or infamous, theory of the mind is the subject of this essay. The next chapter will explain his arguments for the non-material nature of the thinking self, and the paradoxes and tensions which his 'dualistic' theory creates. The final chapter will discuss the fascinating insights arising from his (much lesser known) attempts to resolve those paradoxes and to show how, despite their distinctness, the spiritual self and the mechanical body are intimately *united*, so as to constitute what Descartes called a 'genuine human being'. But first it will be useful to give a brief account of the life and work of that remarkable Frenchman who is so aptly known as 'the father of modern philosophy'.

Life and works

Descartes was born on 31 March 1596 in a small town between Tours and Poitiers, then called La Haye, but now renamed after its greatest son. His mother died when he was thirteen months old, and he was brought up by his maternal grandmother; his father remarried when he was four. At the age of ten, he was sent away to boarding school at the Jesuit college of La Flèche (between Angers and Le Mans). A sickly child, he was given the privilege of 'lying in' in the mornings, a habit that remained with him all his life. In 1610 (aged fourteen) he took part in a lavish ceremony commemorating the death of the college's founder, Henry IV, and among the recitations arranged for the occasion was a poem heralding Galileo's discovery, earlier that same year, of the moons of Jupiter. That the Earth was the centre

7

of all motion had been a central doctrine of the scholastic philosophy, based on a synthesis of Aristotle and the Bible, which had long formed the basis of the curriculum in most schools and universities. But the old order was beginning to crumble.

As a young man, Descartes used the opportunity of volunteering for military service to travel around Europe, and one of the most important experiences of this formative period was his friendship with the Dutch mathematician Isaac Beeckman, whom he met by chance in Breda, in the Netherlands, in 1618. Beeckman, who called himself a 'physico-mathematician', was working on micro-mechanical models of scientific explanation, and he inspired Descartes with enthusiasm for the idea that mathematics, so far from being a purely abstract subject unconnected with the real world, could be employed in the solution of countless problems in physics. Here are some extracts from the letters Descartes wrote to Beeckman early the following year:

> I have received your letter, which I was expecting. On first glancing over it, I was delighted to see your notes on music. What clearer evidence could there be that you had not forgotten me? But there was something else I was looking for, and that the most important, namely news about what you have been doing, what you are doing, and how you are. You ought not to think that all I care about is science; I care about you – and not just your intellect, even if that is the greatest part of you, but the whole man …
>
> Let me be quite open with you about my project.

What I want to produce is ... a completely new science, which would provide a general solution of all possible equations involving any sort of quantity, whether continuous or discrete, each according to its nature ... I am hoping to demonstrate what sort of problems can be solved exclusively in this ... way, so that almost nothing in geometry will remain to be discovered. This is of course a gigantic task, one hardly suitable for a single person; indeed, it is an incredibly ambitious project. But through the confusing darkness I have caught a glimpse of some sort of light, and with the aid of this I think I shall be able to dispel even the thickest obscurities ...

Do not expect anything from my Muse at the moment, for while I am preparing for the journey about to begin tomorrow, my mind has already set out on the voyage. I am still uncertain 'where fate may take me, where my foot may rest'. The preparations for war have not yet led to my being summoned to Germany, but I suspect that many men will be called to arms ... If I should stop somewhere, as I hope I shall, I promise to see that my *Mechanics* or *Geometry* is put in order, and I will salute you as the promoter and prime author of my studies.

For it was you alone who roused me from my state of indolence and reawakened the learning which by then had almost disappeared from my memory; and when my mind strayed from serious pursuits it was you who led it back to worthier things. Thus, if perhaps I should produce something not wholly to be despised, you can rightly claim it all as your own ... (AT X 151–64: CSMK 1–4).

The impending journey to which Descartes refers took him to southern Germany, where on the night of 10 November 1619, he found himself in lodgings at Ulm, on the Danube. It was the eve of St Martin's day, a time of painful childhood memories for Descartes; every year on that evening, in his native region of France, crowds would process though the darkened streets to commemorate the souls of the departed – surely a distressing experience for a small boy who had lost his mother very early in life. Now aged twenty-three, Descartes suffered what some have interpreted as a nervous breakdown, while others, taking their cue from his own more positive interpretation of events, have construed as the real start of his philosophical career. This is how his seventeenth-century biographer, Adrien Baillet, describes it, drawing on records based on Descartes' own notes:

> He went to bed 'quite filled with mental excitement' and preoccupied with the thought that that day he had 'discovered the foundations of a wonderful system of knowledge'. He then had three consecutive dreams, which he imagined could only have come from above. First he was assailed with the impression of several phantoms, which came up to him and terrified him to such an extent that (thinking himself to be walking along a street) he was obliged to cross over onto the left side, in order to get to where he wanted to go; for he felt such a great weakness on his right side that he could not stand up. Being embarrassed to walk in such a fashion, he made an effort to stand upright, but he felt a violent wind which swept him round in a kind of whirlpool,

making him spin round three or four times on his left foot. But this was still not what terrified him most. The difficulty which he had in standing made him believe that he would fall down at each step, until he noticed a College that opened onto his road, and went in to find a refuge and a remedy for his trouble. He tried to reach the college chapel, where his first thought was to go and pray; but noticing that he had passed someone whom he knew without greeting him, he decided to turn back to pay his respects, and was violently pushed back by the wind which blew against the chapel. At the same time, he saw in the middle of the college quadrangle someone else, who addressed him by name in very civil and obliging terms, and told him that if he wanted to look for Monsieur N., he had something to give him. He imagined that this was a melon brought from some foreign country. But what surprised him more was to see that the people who gathered round the man to talk were upright and steady on their feet, while, on the same ground, he was still bent double and reeling, although the wind which had tried to blow him over several times had much lessened ...

Another dream came to him in which he thought he heard a loud and violent noise which he took for a thunderclap. The terror which he felt at this woke him up at once, and opening his eyes he saw many fiery sparks scattered throughout the room ...

Shortly afterwards he had a third dream, which contained nothing terrible like the first two. He found a book on his table, though without knowing who had put it there. He opened it and, seeing that it was an

11

encyclopedia, he was struck with the hope that it might be very useful to him. At the same instant he found another book ... a collection of the poems of different authors entitled *Corpus Poetarum*. He was curious to read something, and opening the book he came to the verse *Quod vitae sectabor iter?* ['What road in life shall I follow?'] At the same instant he saw a man whom he did not know, but who gave him a piece of verse beginning *Est et Non* ... The first book then appeared once more at the other end of the table, but he found that the *Encylopedia* was no longer complete, as it had been when he saw it before.

Beginning to interpret the dream while still asleep, he considered that the encyclopedia signified all the sciences collected together, and that the anthology of poetry indicated philosophy and wisdom combined ... He then woke up quite calmly and continued the interpretation of his dream. The collected poets he took to signify revelation and enthusiasm, with which he had some hope of seeing himself blessed. The piece of verse *Est et Non* – the 'yes and no' of Pythagoras – he took to stand for truth and falsity in human knowledge ... (Adrien Baillet, *La Vie de Monsieur Des-Cartes* [1691], Bk I, ch. 1).

Many rival interpretations have been offered of these strange dreams, including psychoanalytic ones (in some of which, unsurprisingly, the 'melon' figures as a sexual symbol); but from a philosophical point of view it is not hard to see in the whirlpool-like wind of the first dream the kind of disorientation associated with the collapse of confidence in previously accepted certainties. This is precisely the scenario of the philosophical masterpiece Descartes was to compose some twenty years later – the *Meditations* – at the start of which the author decides to doubt all his previous beliefs in a search for the foundations of a new system of knowledge. 'So serious are the doubts into which I have been thrown', he declares at the start of the Second Meditation, 'that I can neither put them out of my mind nor see any way of resolving them. It feels as if I have fallen unexpectedly into a deep whirlpool which tumbles me around so that I can neither stand on the bottom nor swim up to the top' (AT VII 16: CSM II 23–4). As for the 'revelation and enthusiasm' of the poets, this is not normally an image associated with philosophical inquiry; but Descartes clearly believed as a result of his final dream that he was destined to complete the unfinished 'encyclopedia' of the sciences, starting with the 'gigantic project' he had outlined in his earlier letter to Beeckman. In his *Discourse on the Method*, when reflecting some fourteen years later on the thoughts that came to him in the 'stove-heated room', Descartes wrote that 'those long chains of very simple and easy reasonings, which geometers use to arrive at their most difficult demonstrations, gave me occasion to suppose that all the things which come within human knowledge are interconnected in the same way' (*Discourse*, Pt II, AT VI 19: CSM I 120). And just as the poet traditionally claimed divine inspiration, so the clear guiding light of divine truth – always a central feature of Descartes' mature metaphysics – will illuminate the mind of the philosopher. The 'light of reason', or 'natural light' as Descartes came to call it, is nothing 'revelatory' in the biblical sense; on the contrary, it is the austerely intellectual faculty bestowed on us by God which enables us to grasp as self-evident the fundamental mathematical and logical truths that are the key to understanding the universe:

> I always remained firm in the resolution I had taken ... to accept nothing as true which did not seem to me clearer and more certain than the demonstrations of the geometers ... And I noticed certain laws which God has so established in nature, and of which he has implanted such notions in our minds, that after adequate reflection we cannot doubt that they are exactly observed in everything that exists or occurs in the world (*Discourse*, Pt V, AT VI 41: CSM I 131).

After his travels, Descartes lived for a time in Paris, but decided at the age of thirty-two to settle in the Netherlands, where he lived for the next twenty years, though without staying in any one place for very long. His residences included Franeker, Amsterdam, Deventer, Leiden, Haarlem, Utrecht and Endegeest; his favourite retreat was the countryside in the northern coastal area around Egmond, between Haarlem and Alkmaar. His first major work, the *Regulae ad directionem ingenii* (*Rules for the Direction of our Native Intelligence*) was written before he left for Holland, but abandoned unfinished and not published in his lifetime. Also unpublished was his treatise on cosmology and physics *Le Monde* (*The World*), which was ready for the press by 1633, when Descartes suffered an unexpected blow. As he explained in a letter written at the end of November that year to his friend and chief correspondent Marin Mersenne:

I had intended to send you my *World* as a New Year gift, and only two weeks ago I was quite determined to send you at least a part of it, if the whole work could not be copied in time. But I have to say that in the meantime I took the trouble to inquire in Leiden and Amsterdam whether Galileo's *World System* was available, for I thought I had heard that it was published in Italy last year. I was told that it had indeed been published, but that all the copies had immediately been burnt at Rome, and that Galileo had been convicted and fined. I was so astonished at this that I almost decided to burn all my papers, or at least to let no one see them. For I could not imagine that he – an Italian and, as I understand, in the good graces of the Pope – could have been made a criminal for any other reason than that he tried, as he no doubt did, to establish that the Earth moves. I know that some Cardinals had already censured this view, but I thought I had heard it said that all the same it was being taught publicly even in Rome. I must admit that if the view is false, so too are the entire foundations of my philosophy, for it can be demonstrated from them quite clearly. And it is so closely interwoven in every part of my treatise that I could not remove it without rendering the whole work defective. But for all the world I did not want to publish a discourse in which a single word could be found that the Church would have disapproved of; so I preferred to suppress it rather than to publish it in a mutilated form ... (AT I 270–2: CSMK 40–1).

Other works, however, followed thick and fast, beginning with the *Discourse on the Method*, published (in French) together with three scientific essays in 1637, and followed closely by the *Meditations*, which appeared (in Latin) in 1641. The *Principles of Philosophy*, a massive compendium of Cartesian metaphysics and science, came out (in Latin) in 1644. These works, as we shall see, contain Descartes' central arguments for the distinction between mind and body. During the middle 1640s, however, Descartes became increasingly interested in the *interaction* between mind and body, prompted by the acute questions put to him in a long correspondence with Princess Elizabeth of Bohemia (who first wrote to him about his theory of the mind in May 1643). In his replies to Elizabeth, Descartes explores the paradox that while philosophical reason teaches us that mind and body are distinct, our everyday human experience shows us they are united. It is that human experience, and its characteristic modes of awareness, the emotions and passions (such as fear, anger, and love), that forms the subject of Descartes' last work, the *Passions of the Soul*, published in French in 1649.

The same year Descartes accepted, after much hesitation, an invitation by Queen Christina of Sweden to visit her court in Stockholm and instruct her in his philosophy. The decision proved disastrous. In one of his last letters, written in Stockholm on 15 January 1650 to a recently acquired friend, the Comte de Brégy, the philosopher gives voice to his gloom:

> I have seen the Queen only four or five times, always in the morning in her library … A fortnight ago she went to Uppsala, but I did not go with her, nor have I seen her since she returned on Thursday evening. I know also that

our ambassador saw her only once before her visit to Uppsala, apart from his first audience at which I was present. I have not made any other visits, nor have I heard about any. This makes me think that during the winters men's thoughts are frozen here, like the water ... I swear to you that my desire to return to my solitude grows stronger with each passing day ... It is not that I do not still fervently wish to serve the Queen, or that she does not show me as much goodwill as I may reasonably hope for. But I am not in my element here. I desire only peace and quiet, which are benefits that the most powerful monarchs on earth cannot give to those who are unable to acquire them for themselves. I pray God that you are granted the good things that you desire, and I beg you to be assured that I am, Sir, your most humble and obedient servant, Descartes (AT V 466–7: CSMK 383–4).

Within less than a month of writing the letter, just short of his fifty-fourth birthday, Descartes was dead, from a flu-like illness which rapidly produced pneumonia – something the medical resources of the day were utterly unable to cope with. His last words, encapsulating the mind–body dualism which he had so long maintained, were 'Now my soul, 'tis time to depart.'

2
THE INCORPOREAL MIND

Systematic doubt and the nature of the self
Descartes first expounded his theory of mind, and indeed his metaphysics in general, in the context of an engaging personal narrative, where he describes his intellectual development following the momentous day and night in the 'stove-heated room':

> Throughout the next nine years, I did nothing but roam about in the world, trying to be a spectator rather than an actor in all the comedies that are played out there. Reflecting especially upon the points in every subject which might make it suspect and give occasion for us to make mistakes, I kept uprooting from my mind any errors that might previously have slipped into it. In doing this, I was not copying the sceptics, who doubt only for the sake of doubting and pretend to be always undecided; on the contrary, my whole aim was to reach certainty – to cast aside the loose earth and sand so as to come upon rock or clay.
>
> In this I think I was quite successful. For I tried to expose the falsity or uncertainty of the propositions I was examining by clear and certain argument, not by weak conjectures ... And just as in pulling down an old house we usually keep the remnants for use in building a new one, so in destroying all those opinions of mine that I

judged ill-founded, I made various observations and acquired many experiences which I have since used in establishing more certain opinions ...

Those nine years passed by, however, without my taking any side regarding the questions which are commonly debated among the learned, or beginning to search for the foundations of any philosophy more certain than the commonly accepted one ... Exactly eight years ago ... [I resolved] to move away from any place where I might have acquaintances and retire to this country [Holland] ... Living here amidst this great mass of busy people who are more concerned with their own affairs than curious about those of others, I have been able to lead a life as solitary and withdrawn as if I were in the most removed desert, while lacking none of the comforts found in the most populous cities (AT VI 28–31: CSM I 125–6).

Thus ends Part Three of the *Discours de la méthode* (*Discourse on the Method*), published anonymously in 1637. The passage that immediately follows, at the start of Part Four, is one of the most famous in all philosophy, containing the celebrated dictum *je pense donc je suis* – 'I think therefore I am' – or (perhaps closer to Descartes' meaning) 'I am thinking, therefore I exist.' The *Discourse* was translated into Latin seven years later (Latin, in the seventeenth century, still being the best way to reach an international audience), and there the dictum appears in what is probably still its best known form: *Cogito ergo sum*.

The full title of the *Discourse* is 'Discourse on the Method of rightly conducting one's reason and seeking the truth in the sciences', and one key to the 'method' in question is Descartes' deliberate use of the techniques (though not the philosophical outlook) of scepticism, pushing doubt as far as it will go. The purpose is to see whether there is anything at all that *survives* the doubt: if so, it will serve as the foundation stone for the new reliable edifice of science that Descartes is seeking to construct. The first truth that Descartes proceeds to discover is, of course, the famous *Cogito* – so long as I am thinking, I must exist – and commentators have endlessly analysed and debated the precise significance of the 'Archimedian point' on which Descartes proposes to rely in order to launch the rest of his system. But more interesting for our purposes is the move Descartes makes immediately following the Cogito, where he goes on to dicuss the *nature* of this thinking being of whose existence he is so sure. Here is the opening of Part Four of the *Discourse* in full:

I do not know whether I should tell you of the first meditations that I had there, for they are perhaps too metaphysical and uncommon for everyone's taste. And yet, to make it possible to judge whether the foundations I have chosen are firm enough, I am in a way obliged to speak of them. For a long time I had observed … that in practical life it is sometimes necessary to follow opinions which one knows to be quite uncertain, just as one would if they were indubitable. But since I now wished to devote myself solely to the search for truth, I thought it necessary to do the very opposite and reject, treating as absolutely false, everything in which I could imagine the least doubt, in order to see if I was left believing anything that was entirely indubitable.

Thus, because our senses sometimes deceive us, I decided to suppose that nothing was such as they had led us to imagine. And because there are people who make mistakes in reasoning and commit logical fallacies even about the simplest matters in geometry, judging that I was as prone to error as anyone else I rejected as unsound all the arguments I had previously taken as demonstrative proofs. Lastly, considering that the very thoughts we have while awake may also occur while we are asleep, without any of them being, at the time, true, I resolved to pretend that all the things that had ever entered my mind were no truer than the illusions of my dreams. But immediately I noticed that while I was trying in this way to think that everything was false, it was necessary that I, who was thinking this, was something. And observing that this truth *'I am thinking, therefore I exist'* was so firm and sure that even the most extravagant suppositions of the sceptics were incapable of shaking it, I decided I could accept it without scruple as the first principle of the philosophy I was seeking.

Next, I examined attentively *what* I was. I saw that while I could pretend I had no body and that there was no world and no place for me to be in, I could not for all that pretend that *I* did not exist. I saw on the contrary that from the mere fact that I thought of doubting the truth of other things, it followed quite evidently and certainly that I existed; yet if I had but ceased to think, even if everything else I had ever imagined were true, this would have left me no reason whatever to believe I existed. From this I recognized that I was a substance whose whole essence or nature is solely to think, and which does not require any place, or depend on any material thing, in order to exist. Accordingly this 'I' – that is, the soul by which I am what I am – is entirely distinct from the body, and indeed is easier to know than the body, and would not cease to be everything it is even if the body did not exist (AT VI 31–3: CSM I 126–7).

The final paragraph contains Descartes' first attempt (he produced other arguments in later works) to prove the immaterial nature of the mind. It is important, incidentally, not to be put off by the faintly religious or 'spiritual' modern overtones of the term 'soul', which appears in the concluding sentence. Descartes uses *l'âme* ('soul') and *l'esprit* ('mind') more or less interchangeably, simply to refer to whatever it is that is conscious, or thinks – the 'thinking thing' (*res cogitans*) as he later calls it in the *Meditations*. And his conclusion, here in the *Discourse* as in the later works, is that the conscious thinking self – 'This "I" (*ce moi*) by which I am what I am' – is entirely independent of anything physical, and indeed could survive the complete destruction of the body (including, let us be clear, the brain).

At the turn of the twentieth century, when scientists are almost every month discovering more about the chemical and electrical processes going on in the brain during thought, Descartes' position may initially strike some people as bizarre or even ridiculous. But Descartes does not deny that thought in human beings may be *accompanied* by brain processes (indeed, he spent a great deal of time discussing the physiology of the brain and nervous system); what he insists is that thought is not to be *identified* with these or any other physical processes, since it is, in its essential nature, distinct from the material realm, and indeed is in principle capable of existing without any physical substrate whatsoever.

The key premise for understanding Descartes' argument is the statement, 'I could pretend I had no body.' This clearly links up with the technique of doubt Descartes has described earlier on. Consider a proposition about a bodily movement, for example, 'I am stretching out my hand.' Well, however simple and obvious truths such as this may seem, they can, with enough determination and ingenuity, be doubted: I might be asleep and dreaming, in which case I am not stretching out my hand at all, but (for example) lying in bed with my hands pillowed under my ear. This level of 'the dreaming argument', however, still admits that I have a body. Yet Descartes is prepared to push the doubt one stage further: maybe 'all the things that have *ever entered my mind*' are 'no truer than the illusions of my dreams' (middle paragraph of passage quoted above). Perhaps, in other words, the whole of life might be some sort of dream, including the belief that I have a body. Or to use the more dramatic scenario which Descartes introduced four years later, in the *Meditations*:

> I will suppose that ... some malicious demon of the utmost power and cunning has employed all his energies in order to deceive me. I shall think that the sky, the air, the earth, colours, shapes, sounds and *all external things* are merely the delusions of dreams which he has

devised to ensnare my judgement. I shall consider myself
as not having hands or eyes or flesh or blood or senses,
but as falsely believing that I have all these things ... (AT
VII 22–3: CSM II 15).

This extreme form of doubt enables me to suspend belief in
all 'external' things – that is, everything apart from the
direct and immediate flow of my thoughts. Conclusion: I
may not have a body at all; I may be some kind of bodiless
spirit mercilessly tricked by the wicked demon into thinking I am a creature of flesh and blood living on planet
Earth. Yet even pushing doubt to these exaggerated or
'hyperbolical' limits (as Descartes himself called them), I
nevertheless cannot doubt that *I* exist. Even if I am the
dupe of the demon, I must exist for him to be able to
deceive me. This is how Descartes takes up the story in the
Second Meditation:

> I will suppose that everything I see is spurious. I will
> believe that my memory tells me lies, and that none of
> the things that it reports ever happened. I have no
> senses. Body, shape, extension, movement and place
> are chimeras. So what remains true? ...
>
> I have just said that I have no senses and no body. This
> is the sticking point: what follows from this? Am I not so
> bound up with a body and with senses that I cannot
> exist without them? But I have convinced myself that
> there is absolutely nothing in the world, no sky, no
> earth, no minds, no bodies. Does it follow that I too do
> not exist? No! If I convinced myself of something then I
> certainly existed. But there is a deceiver of supreme

power and cunning who is deliberately and constantly deceiving me. In that case I too undoubtedly exist, if he is deceiving me. And let him deceive me as much as he can, he will never bring it about that I am nothing so long as I think I am something (AT VII 24–5: CSM II 16–17).

So the existence of my own conscious self is utterly indubitable: unlike the body, it is immune even to the most extreme doubts that can be devised.

But even if we go along with Descartes here, can we accept the result he deduces from all this? He has established that I can doubt the existence of my body, but not that of my mind or my conscious self: very well, but does it follow, in the words of the *Discourse*, that this 'I' is 'entirely distinct from the body' and could exist without it? To answer this we must look at the *logical form* of Descartes' argument, which appears to be as follows:

> I can doubt the existence of B
> But I cannot doubt the existence of M
> So M could exist without B

Now if this form of argument were valid, it would be valid not just for Mind and Body, but for all substitutions of M and B. Yet consider the following analogy. Let M be Mashed potato, and B be carBohydrate. Suppose (being utterly ignorant of chemistry) I can doubt the existence of carbohydrate; yet suppose also, for the sake of argument, that I am incapable of doubting the existence of this mashed potato that is being rammed down my throat. Does it follow, to parody Descartes, that the mashed potato could still exist, and 'would not fail to be what it is', even if carbohydrate did not exist?

Descartes' mistake seems to be to try to read off truth about ontology from epistemological truth – or, to put the matter less portentously, to try to deduce conclusions about the *real nature* of the mind or thinking self from premises about what he can or cannot be *certain* of, or can or cannot *doubt*. Yet what I am capable of doubting about any given item seems to depend partly on the extent of my own familiarity with that item. And the extent of my own familiarity, with minds, or potatoes, or anything else, seems a poor basis for reaching firm conclusions about what is really essential or inessential to their existence.

As to the inherent plausibility of Descartes' conclusion, in identifying 'this "I"' with an incorporeal entity he is certainly departing from what might be called the 'common sense' position. Most people asked the question 'What are you?' would presumably reply 'a human being'; and a human being, plainly, is not something incorporeal but, as Aristotle put it, a 'rational animal', a certain sort of biological creature, and therefore very much a creature of flesh and blood. Descartes acknowledges, in the Second Meditation, that his view is a departure from the 'first thought to come to mind':

> I do not yet have a sufficient understanding of what this 'I' is that now necessarily exists. So I must be on my guard against carelessly taking something else to be this 'I' and so making a mistake in the very item of knowledge that I maintain is the most certain and evident of all. I will therefore go back and meditate on

what I originally believed myself to be, before I embarked on this present train of thought. I will then subtract anything capable of being weakened, even minimally, by the arguments now introduced, so that what is left at the end may be exactly and only what is certain and unshakeable.

What then did I formerly think I was ... Well, the first thought to come to mind was that I had a face, hands, arms, and the whole mechanical structure of limbs which can be seen in a corpse and which I called 'the body'. The next thought was that I was nourished, that I moved about, and that I engaged in sense perception and thinking ...

But what shall I now say that I am, when I am supposing that there is some supremely powerful and ... malicious deceiver who is deliberately trying to trick me in every way he can? Can I now assert that I possess even the most insignificant of all the attributes which I have just said belong to the nature of a body? I scrutinize them, think about them, go over them again, but nothing suggests itself; it is tiresome and pointless to repeat the list once more. But what about ... nutrition and movement? Since now I do not have a body, these are mere fabrications. Sense perception? This surely does not occur without a body, and besides, when asleep I have appeared to perceive through the senses many things which I have afterwards realized I did not perceive through the senses at all. Thinking? At last I have discovered it – thought. *This alone is inseparable from me.* I am, I exist – that is certain. But for how long? For as long as I am thinking. For it could be that were I totally to cease from thinking, I should totally cease to exist. At present I am not admitting anything except what is necessarily true. *I am, then, in the strict sense only a thing that thinks*; that is, I am a mind, or intelligence, or intellect or reason – words whose meaning I have been ignorant of until now. But for all that I am a thing which is real and which truly exists. But what kind of a thing? As I have just said, a thinking thing (AT VII 25–7: CSM II 17–18).

Thought, this reasoning claims, is the only attribute that cannot be separated from me by the extreme doubts raised in the demon scenario: it is the only thing that cannot be 'torn away from me' (*divelli*), as the original Latin has it. Yet this seems to beg some questions. If, as many people now believe, brain activity is in fact essential to thought, then how does this affect the imaginary scenario where I am supposed to be a bodiless creature deceived by the demon into thinking I have a body? The answer must surely be that the alleged scenario is incoherent; for in 'tearing off' the brain and all the other bodily attributes, one would thereby be 'tearing off' thought as well. As Descartes' acute contemporary Antoine Arnauld put it, summing up his enduring worries about the argument, for all Descartes has shown it could still be that the body is, after all, essential to what makes me 'me':

So far as I can see, the only result that follows is that I can obtain some knowledge of myself without knowledge of the body. But it is not yet transparently clear to me that this knowledge is complete and adequate, *so as to enable me to be certain that I am not mistaken in*

28

excluding body from my essence (Fourth Replies, AT VII
201: CSM II 141).

'Clear and distinct perception' and the logical possibility of disembodied minds

Soon after writing the *Discourse*, Descartes became all too
aware of problems in his argument from doubt for the
immateriality of the mind. As he explained in the Preface to
the *Meditations*, published in 1641:

In the *Discourse*, I asked anyone who found anything
worth criticizing in what I had written to be kind enough
to point it out to me. In the case of my remarks
concerning ... the soul, only [one objection] worth
mentioning was put to me, which I shall now briefly
answer ...

The ... objection is this. From the fact that the human
mind, when directed towards itself, does not perceive
itself to be anything other than a thinking thing, it does
not follow that its nature or essence consists *only* in its
being a thinking thing, where the word 'only' excludes
everything else that could be said to belong to the
nature of the soul. My answer to this objection is that in
that passage it was not my intention to make those
exclusions in an order corresponding to the actual truth
of the matter (which I was not dealing with at that
stage) but merely in an order corresponding to my own
perception. So the sense of the passage was that I was
aware of nothing at all that I *knew* belonged to my
essence, except that I was a thinking thing, or a thing
possessing within itself the faculty of thinking. I shall,

however, show below how it follows from the fact that I am unaware of nothing else belonging to my essence, that *nothing else does in fact belong to it* (AT VII 7–8: CSM II 7).

Although, as we have already seen, the Second Meditation repeats much of the reasoning of the *Discourse*, the promised additional argument makes its appearance in the Sixth (and final) Meditation. The argument, as Descartes presents it, depends heavily on his proofs of God's existence, and hence (since the proofs in question are widely regarded as invalid) has not perhaps received as much attention as it deserves; as we shall see shortly, however, there is what might be called a 'secular analogue' of the argument, which many present-day philosophers, even anti-Cartesian ones, tend to accept.

To explain how Descartes' argument works some brief stage-setting will be necessary. By the time we reach the Sixth Meditation, the meditator has established, to his own satisfaction, the existence of a perfect creator who has bestowed on the mind its faculty of 'clear and distinct perception', a faculty which, if we use it carefully, cannot lead us astray:

The cause of error must surely be the one I have explained [viz. misusing my free will in rashly giving assent to propositions I do not clearly perceive]. For if, whenever I have to make a judgement, I restrain my will so that it extends to what the intellect clearly and distinctly reveals, and no further, then it is quite impossible for me to go wrong. This is because every clear and distinct perception is undoubtedly something real and positive, and hence cannot come from nothing, but must necessarily have God for its author. Its author, I say, is God, who is supremely perfect and who cannot be a deceiver on pain of contradiction; hence the perception is undoubtedly true. So today I have learned not only what precautions to take to avoid ever going wrong, but also what to do to arrive at the truth. For I shall unquestionably reach the truth if only I give sufficient attention to all the things which I perfectly understand, and separate these from all the other cases where my apprehension is more confused and obscure. And this is just what I shall take good care to do from now on (Fourth Meditation, AT VII 62: CSM II 43).

God, in Descartes' metaphysics, is the bridge from the subjective world of thought to the objective world of scientific truth. The mind, owing its existence to God, is innately programmed with certain ideas that correspond to reality; hence the importance, in Descartes' system, of proving the existence of God, the perfect guarantor of our ideas, so that the meditator can move from isolated flashes of cognition (I am thinking, I exist …) to systematic knowledge of the nature of reality:

I see plainly that the certainty and truth of all knowledge depends uniquely on my awareness of the true God, to such an extent that I was incapable of perfect knowledge about anything else until I became aware of him. And now it is possible for me to achieve full and certain knowledge of countless matters, both concerning God himself and other things whose nature is intellectual, and also concerning that whole of that corporeal nature which is the subject matter of pure mathematics (Fifth Meditation, AT VII 71: CSM II 49).

Having opened up the possibility of systematic knowledge of the real natures of things, via the (divinely guaranteed) clear and distinct perceptions of the intellect, this is how Descartes proceeds in the Sixth Meditation to argue for the distinctness of mind and body.

> I know that everything which I clearly and distinctly understand is capable of being created by God so as to correspond exactly with my understanding of it. Hence the fact that I can clearly and distinctly understand one thing apart from another is enough to make me certain that the two things are distinct, since they are *capable of being separated*, at least by God. The question of what kind of power is required to bring about such a separation does not affect the judgement that the two things are distinct.
>
> Thus, simply by knowing that I exist, and noticing at the same time that absolutely nothing else belongs to my nature of essence except that I am a thinking thing, I can infer correctly that my essence consists solely in the fact that I am a thinking thing. It is true that I may have (or, to anticipate, certainly have) a body that is very closely joined to me. But nevertheless, on the one hand I have a clear and distinct idea of *myself, in so far as I am simply a thinking, non-extended thing*; and on the other hand I have a distinct idea of *body, in so far as this is simply an extended, non-thinking thing*. And accordingly it is certain that I am really distinct from my body, and can exist without it. (AT VII 78: CSM II 54).

'Extended' things (as explained in the previous chapter) are the subject matter of Cartesian physics; they are defined as whatever has spatial dimensions and hence can be *quantified* or measured in terms of size, shape and motion. The body, and all its organs, including the brain, is clearly 'extended' in this sense; indeed, it seems a contradiction to call anything a 'body' unless it has measurable dimensions. Descartes' premise that he has a clear and distinct idea of body as extended thus seems unexceptionable. Many, moreover, would agree with his further premise that we have a clear and distinct idea of mind as something *un*extended. Certainly, thoughts do not seem to occupy space in the way in which molecules or tables or planets do. Consciousness – the flow of sensations and reflections and desires and cogitations that make up our mental life – seems on the face of it to belong to an entirely separate category from the particles of measurable shape and motion that make up the universe as studied by the physicist. So the notions of mind and of body, let us agree with Descartes, are distinct notions.

Can we get from here to the conclusion that 'I am really distinct from the body and could exist without it?' Descartes' reasoning seems to be that if I can clearly understand the notion of mind without reference to anything extended, and if I can clearly understand the notion of body without reference to anything conscious, then it is at least logically possible that a mind could exist apart from a body. As Descartes puts it, 'they are *capable* of being separated, at least by God'. And if they *can* exist apart, then mind does not depend for its existence on the body, and hence the body is not part of its essential nature.

Notice (to come back to the 'secular analogue' of Descartes' argument hinted at earlier) that this reasoning does not in fact depend on there being a God who creates disembodied souls. The real point of the argument is not that minds *do* exist apart from bodies, but that they are *capable* of so doing. And anyone who concedes this has really conceded the basic plank of Descartes' mind–body dualism. Thus those philosophers nowadays who maintain that in our actual universe all consciousness is embodied in some physical or organic system, but allow that it is at least *logically possible* that there could be purely spiritual entities, existing free from any bodily structure – such philosophers are in fact going along with the main thrust of Cartesian dualism. And it is a very short step from this to agreeing with Descartes that, though your present human life involves both mental and physical attributes, it is possible that your body could be destroyed, and yet the real essential 'you' still survive.

There is, however, another perspective from which Descartes' argument appears more suspect. To approach the question 'Can thought exist without a brain (or some analogous physical structure)?', consider the parallel question: 'Can digestion exist without a stomach (or appropriate alternative physical organs)?' The answer to the second question is surely: no. For although the concepts of digestion and stomach are quite distinct concepts, and we can, as it were, separate them out in our thought, the two are nevertheless intimately related as function is related to structure: the function of digestion, if it is actually to *operate*, must be embodied in a physical structure with the appropriate causal powers (e.g. the ability to process food).

And similarly, it seems plausible to argue that although the concept of thought is quite distinct from the concept of brain activity, thought is nonetheless a *functional* process, which cannot operate without some sort of hardware (either a brain or something analogous). Software engineers, to be sure, design their programs in purely abstract terms, without any reference to the physical world; but they know, nonetheless, that for their programs actually to *operate*, they must be physically embodied (e.g. on a hard disk). For there to be an operating software program in the absence of a physical substrate is, ultimately, an incoherent notion: it is not just that it does not occur in our universe, but that there is no possible world in which it is found (any more than there is a possible world in which there are functioning digestive processes in the absence of some kind of physical organs capable of doing the job). If this is right, then however plausible it might appear at first sight to suppose it is logically possible for there to be minds existing apart from bodies, the notion turns out ultimately to be incoherent, and Descartes' argument thus fails.

The indivisibility of consciousness
Descartes has one more string to his bow in arguing for the distinctness of mind and body. Towards the end of the Sixth Meditation, he makes the following observation:

> There is a great difference between the mind and the body, inasmuch as the body is by its very nature always divisible, while the mind is utterly indivisible. For when I consider the mind, or myself in so far as I am merely a thinking thing, I am unable to distinguish any parts

within myself; I understand myself to be something quite single and complete. Although the whole mind seems to be united to the whole body, I recognize that if a foot or arm or any other part of the body is cut off, nothing has thereby been taken away from the mind. (As for the faculties of willing, of understanding, of sensory perception and so on, these cannot be termed *parts* of the mind, since it is one and the same mind that wills, and understands, and has sensory perceptions.) By contrast there is no corporeal or extended thing that I can think of which in my thought I cannot easily divide into parts; and this very fact makes me understand that it is divisible. This one argument would be enough to show me that the mind is completely different from the body, even if I did not already know as much from other considerations (AT VII 85–6: CSM II 59).

Some of this seems rather inept, as when Descartes talks of the removal of a foot or arm not taking anything from the mind, to which his modern opponents will immediately retort, 'What about the removal of the brain or the nervous system?' Other recent critics have cast doubt on the alleged 'indivisibility' of the mind, pointing out that contemporary research has shown that the alleged unity of consciousness may be an illusion, our mental functioning being in reality an uneasy amalgam of a host of semi-autonomous and often quite loosely co-operating subsystems. But perhaps the most questionable aspect of Descartes' argument is that he already seems tacitly to be 'reifying' the mind – assuming it is an entity or substance in its own right. If, instead, the mind is the name for a set of *functions*, or *attributes*, rather than a substance, then the fact that we cannot divide up and weigh and measure those functions in the way we can divide up and measure portions of the brain is ultimately beside the point. We cannot divide up, measure and weigh the spell-checking function in a word-processor, in the way we can divide up, measure and weigh the hardware; but for all that the wordprocessing function cannot operate except in virtue of the properties of a physical system.

Descartes' arguments, flawed though they may be, do succeed in underlining an important fact about mental phenomena, namely that the quantitative language of physics, involving terms like size, shape, extension, motion and so on, seems wholly inadequate to describe the inner dimension of our mental life. It is this subjective dimension that makes many modern philosophers retain what might be called 'quasi-Cartesian' leanings, even though they have little truck with the notion of independent spiritual sub-stances. However complete our physical science, will it ever be able to encompass what it is like to smell new-mown hay, or to taste a ripe raspberry, or to hear the bagpipes? Such subjective qualitative impressions, or 'qualia', as the jargon now dubs them, are felt by many to be destined to elude for ever the clutches of even the most advanced physics we can conceive of.

It is interesting that examples of such allegedly recalci-trant 'qualia' are generally drawn not from the domain of 'pure thought' – e.g. the thought that two plus two makes four, which seems relatively abstract and 'colourless' from the standpoint of the experiencing subject – but rather from the warm-blooded world of human sensation and emotion. It is to Descartes' treatment of this characteristically human dimension to our mental life that we must now turn.

3
THE TRUE HUMAN BEING

Descartes' rebuttal of 'angelism'
It is one of the great paradoxes of Descartes' philosophical development that, having expended so much energy arguing that mind and body are two distinct and mutually *independent* substances, he spent a large part of the final decade of his life insisting on their *interdependence* – an interdependence so close and intimate as to amount to what he called a 'real substantial union'. This is not, however, as abrupt a *volte face* as it might seem, since the basic fact of the 'union' between mind and body was something Descartes had already asserted quite unequivocally in the *Meditations*:

> There is nothing that my own nature teaches me more vividly than that I have a body, and that when I feel pain there is something wrong with the body, and that when I am hungry or thirsty the body needs food and drink, and so on ...
>
> Nature also teaches me, by these sensations of pain, hunger, thirst and so on, that I am not merely *present* in my body as a sailor is present in a ship, but that I am *very closely joined and, as it were, intermingled with it, so that I and the body form a unit*. If this were not so, I, who am nothing but a thinking thing, would not feel pain when the body was hurt, but would perceive the

damage purely by the intellect, just as a sailor perceives by sight if anything in his ship is broken. Similarly, when the body needed food or drink, I should have an explicit understanding of the fact, instead of having confused sensations of hunger and thirst. For the sensations of hunger, thirst, pain and so on are nothing but confused modes of thinking which arise from the *union and, as it were, intermingling* of the mind with the body (Sixth Meditation, AT VII 80–1: CSM II 56).

What would life be like for a pure disembodied spirit that happened to be implanted into a body? The body, being alien to its essential nature, would simply be a piece of apparatus, or a vehicle, Descartes suggests; and hence damage to the body would be perceived rather as I perceive that my car has been dented, or the roof of my house is leaking: the mind would simply record these facts as 'external' to itself – inconvenient, to be sure, but not directly and immediately involving its very being, as happens when a human feels bodily distress as the result of illness or injury. In the latter case, it is not just that I make the judgement: 'What a nuisance, this body I am using is damaged'; rather I *feel*, in a peculiarly direct and intimate way, that acute and obtrusive sensation we all know as pain. And it is this 'confused mode of thinking', Descartes argues, that is a sure sign that mind and body are not just related as sailor to ship, or passenger to vehicle, but are closely 'united' and 'intermingled'.

Why does Descartes call sensations like pain *confused* thoughts? Part of the reason is that they lack the clarity and distinctness of which intellectual perceptions are capable. When I judge that two and two make four, or that a triangle has three sides, the content of my thought is transparently clear to the understanding, and I have – right in front of me as it were – everything that is necessary for me to be certain of the truth of the proposition in question. By contrast, there is for Descartes something inherently opaque about the sensory data we receive when the body is stimulated in various ways. The feelings are vivid and intense enough, but there are not the same transparent logical connections that are manifest when the intellect is contemplating clear and distinct propositions like those of mathamatics:

As for the body which by some special right I called 'mine', my belief that this body, more than any other, belonged to me has some justification. For I could never be separated from it, as I could from other bodies; and I felt all my appetites and emotions in, and on account of, this body; and finally, I was aware of pain and pleasurable tickling in parts of this body, but not in other bodies external to it. But why should that curious sensation of pain give rise to a particular distress of mind; or why should a certain kind of delight follow on a tickling sensation? Again, why should that curious tugging in the stomach which I call hunger tell me that I should eat, or a dryness of the throat tell me to drink, and so on? I was not able to give any explanation of all this, except that nature taught me so. For there is absolutely no connection (at least that I can understand) between the tugging sensation and the decision to take food, or between the sensation of something causing pain and the mental apprehension of distress that arises from that sensation ... (AT VII 76: CSM II 52–3).

It is the *strangeness* of psycho-physical sensations like hunger and pain, their inherent dissimilarity from the transparent perceptions of the intellect, that shows us that we are not simply pure minds annexed to bodies. Instead, this particular body is *mine* in a peculiar, yet undeniable and vividly manifested way. This is the characteristic 'signature', as it were, of my existence not just as a 'thinking thing' plugged into a mechanical body, but as that unique amalgam of mind and body, a *human being*.

Commentators, at least the anglophone tradition, have tended to ignore this crucial aspect of Descartes' philosophy, preferring instead to focus on his arguments for the distinctness of mind and body. In the celebrated phrase of the English philosopher Gilbert Ryle (in *The Concept of Mind*, 1949), the Cartesian approach has become synonymous with the doctrine of the 'ghost in the machine' – an immaterial spirit controlling an alien, mechanical body. The charge is not a new one, but is found among Descartes' own contemporaries, who often accused him of reverting to a Platonic-style 'angelism'. Antoine Arnauld, author of the Fourth Set of Objections to the *Meditations*, put it this way:

It seems that the argument [that mind can exist apart from body] proves too much, and takes us back to the Platonic view ... that nothing corporeal belongs to our essence, so that man is merely a rational soul, and the body merely a vehicle to the soul – a view which gives rise to the definition of a human being as *anima corpore* utens ('a soul which makes use of a body') (AT VII 203: CSM II 143).

Descartes briskly replied:

> I do not see why the argument 'proves too much' ... I thought I was very careful to guard against anyone inferring that a human being is simply 'a soul which makes use of a body'. For in the Sixth Meditation, where I dealt with the distinction between the mind and the body, I also proved at the same time that the mind is substantially united with the body. And the arguments which I have used to prove this are as strong as any I can remember ever having read. Now someone who says that a man's arm is a substance that is really distinct from the rest of his body does not thereby deny that the arm belongs to the nature of the whole man. And saying that the arm belongs to the nature of the whole man does not give rise to the suspicion that it cannot subsist in its own right. In the same way, I do not think I proved too much in showing that the mind can exist apart from the body. Nor do I think I proved too little in saying that the mind is substantially united with the body, since that substantial union does not prevent our having a clear and distinct concept of the mind on its own, as a complete thing (AT VII 227–8: CSM II 160).

Descartes' reply is not perhaps as perspicuous as it might be; but the nub of the issue boils down to whether Descartes has a genuine 'anthropology' (Greek *anthropos*, 'human being') – whether he has a theory which does justice to our essential nature as human beings. Following the publication of the *Meditations*, Descartes' over-enthusiastic disciple Regius put it forward as the Cartesian view that the human being was simply a contingent or accidental entity – in the jargon, an *ens per accidens* – something, as it were, that merely happens to come into existence when a soul is joined to a body, but which lacks the status of something with a genuine essence of its own. In a stern letter to him, Descartes thundered, 'You could scarcely have said anything more objectionable and provocative' (AT III 460: CSMK 200). A month later he wrote again in more detail, adamantly rejecting Regius' interpretation, and insisting that the human being is indeed an *ens per se*, a genuine entity in its own right:

> The mind is united in real and substantial manner to the body ... As I said in my *Meditations*, we perceive that sensations such as pain are not pure thoughts of a mind distinct from a body, but confused perceptions of a mind really united to a body. For if an angel were in a human body, it would not have sensations as we do, but would simply perceive the motions which are caused by external objects, and in this way would differ from a *genuine human being* (AT III 493: CSMK 206).

Emphatic though Descartes' reply is, it leaves many questions unanswered. If mind and body are indeed distinct and independent substances, how is it that they can interact and combine; and what exactly is meant by the 'real substantial union' between them? These are questions to which Descartes did not give systematic further attention until he was challenged to explain himself more fully by perhaps his most famous correspondent, the Princess Elizabeth, daughter of Frederick, the exiled King of Bohemia, and niece of the ill-fated Charles I of England.

'Primitive notions' and the substantial union

Princess Elizabeth wrote to Descartes in May 1642 asking him how the soul, being simply a 'thinking substance', can initiate the relevant events in the nervous system so as to produce voluntary movements of the limbs (a highly pertinent question, anticipating Gilbert Ryle's attack, three hundred years later, on the idea of a Cartesian 'ghost' supposedly able to move a corporeal 'machine'). Descartes replied with unusual candour:

> I may truly say that the question Your Highness poses seems to me the one which can most properly be put to me in view of my published writings. There are two facts about the human soul on which depend all the knowledge we can have of its nature. The first is that it thinks; the second is that, being united to the body, it can act and be acted upon along with it. About the second I have said hardly anything; I have tried only to make the first well understood. For my principal aim was to prove the *distinction* between the soul and the body, and to this end only the first was useful, and the second might have been harmful. But because Your Highness's vision is so clear that nothing can be concealed from her, I will try now to explain how I conceive the *union* of the soul and the body, and how the soul has the power to move the body.
>
> First, I consider that there are in us certain primitive

notions which are as it were the patterns on the basis of which we form all our other conceptions ... As regards body in particular we have only the notion of extension, which entails the notions of shape and motion; as regards the soul on its own, we have only the notion of thought, which includes the perceptions of the intellect and the inclinations of the will. Lastly, as regards the soul and the body together, we have only the notion of their *union*, on which depends our notion of the soul's power to move the body and the body's power to act on the soul and cause its sensations and passions (letter of 21 May 1643, AT 664–5: CSMK 217–18).

This does not do much to explain how mind and body are able to interact, but Descartes was later to deny that this was, in itself, a problem: 'It is a false supposition ... that if the soul and the body are two substances whose nature is different, this prevents them from being able to act on each other' (AT IXA 213: CSM II 275). The most striking aspect of his comments to Elizabeth, however, is that Descartes makes no attempt to use the somewhat obscure jargon he had employed in dealing with Regius ('accidental entity' versus 'entity in its own right'), but instead makes the remarkable claim that the concept of the human being, the mind–body union, is a *primitive notion*. On the face of it this is quite mysterious: 'primitive' suggests 'basic', or 'not further analysable'; yet if the union is made up of body plus soul, elsewhere declared to be the fundamental categories of Cartesian metaphysics, how can the amalgam of the two be apprehended by a 'primitive notion'? It is as if a chemist were to say the concept of water is a 'primitive' one, but then go on to add that water is made up of the more basic substances, hydrogen and oxygen.

In response to further probing by Elizabeth, Descartes wrote to her again a month later:

> I observe one great difference between these three kinds of notion. The soul is conceived only by the pure intellect; body (i.e. extension, shapes and motions) can likewise be known by the intellect alone, but much better by the intellect aided by the imagination; and finally what belongs to the union of the soul and the body is known only obscurely by the intellect alone, or even by the intellect aided by the imagination, but it is known very clearly by the senses. That is why people who never philosophize and use only their senses have no doubt that the soul moves the body and that the body acts on the soul. They regard both of them as a single thing, that is to say, they conceive their union; because to conceive the union between two things is to conceive them as one single thing. Metaphysical thoughts, which exercise the pure intellect, help to familiarise us with the notion of the soul; and the study of mathematics, which exercises mainly the imagination in the consideration of shapes and motions, accustoms us to form very distinct notions of body. But it is the ordinary course of life and conversation, and abstention from meditation and from the study of the things which exercise the imagination, that teaches us how to conceive the union of the soul and the body (letter of 28 June 1643, AT III 691–2: CSMK 226–7).

The passage is a strange one, since it almost seems to

abdicate the role of the philosopher: stop trying to *analyse* the union, Descartes seems to be telling Elizabeth; it is enough that we *feel* it, in our day-to-day sensory experience. The difficulty here is what seems to be an admission that our ordinary experience is actually inconsistent with Descartes' official mind–body dualism: his philosophical arguments have purported to show that there are two distinct entities here, but he now appears to concede that our ordinary experience reveals a single, united being. The impression of a serious philosophical impasse is reinforced in the following paragraph:

> I think it was [philosophical meditations] rather than thoughts requiring less attention that have made Your Highness find obscurity in the notion we have of the union of the mind and the body. It does not seem to me that the human mind is capable of forming a very distinct conception of both the distinction between the soul and the body, and their union; for to do this it is necessary to conceive of them as a single thing and at the same time to conceive of them as two things, and the two conceptions are mutually opposed (AT III 693: CSMK 227).

Some have taken this to be throwing in the towel and admitting the whole theory of the union of distinct substances is incoherent. The way forward, however, is to focus on those attributes which Descartes always refers to when discussing the mind–body union: the emotions, feelings and passions. These are modalities of awareness that are unique to the human mind–body composite, and it is here, it seems to me, that the 'primitiveness' of the notion of the union is to be explained.

In insisting that we have a 'primitive notion' of the union of mind and body, alongside our primitive notions of thought and of extension, Descartes should be understood as asserting that the mind–body complex is something which is the bearer of *distinctive and irreducible properties in its own right*. In this sense we might say that water is a 'primitive' notion, meaning that it is not a mere mixture but a genuine compound, possessing attributes 'in its own right' (distinctive 'watery' characteristics that cannot be reduced to the properties of the hydrogen or oxygen which make it up). In the same way, Descartes regards the sensations and passions as not reducible either to pure thought, on the one hand, or to events in the extended world of physics, on the other. That he is on to something important here may be seen from the fact that to experience *hunger* is not reducible either to (i) making the purely intellectual judgement 'I need nourishment', on the one hand, or to (ii) the occurrence of the purely physiological events (stomach contractions, fall in blood sugar) on the other. For example, (i) someone could be drugged into not feeling hungry, yet still make the judgement that he needs to eat, e.g. as a result of calculating the time elapsed since the last meal, or by measuring his blood sugar. And (ii) the physiological events could obviously occur without the experience of hunger – for example, in an anaesthetized patient.

If Descartes' theory of the 'three primitive notions' is supported by the irreducibility of psycho-physical attributes like hunger either to pure thought or to extension, this need not imply any logical clash with his official doctrine of two and only two substances, mind and body. For the 'trialistic' division found in the letters to Elizabeth can, along the lines just suggested, be construed as an *attributive* rather than substantival trialism: the human being is not an additional *substance* alongside mind and body (any more than water is an additional substance in the universe, to be listed alongside hydrogen and oxygen); but what is true is that in virtue of our embodied state, as creatures of flesh and blood, human beings enjoy modes of awareness which (to use Descartes' own language) 'must not be referred either to the mind alone or to the body alone'. This is how Descartes sums it up in Part I article 48 of his *Principles of Philosophy*, published in 1644:

I recognize only *two* ultimate classes of things: first, intellectual or thinking things, i.e. those which pertain to mind or thinking substance; and secondly, material things, i.e. those which pertain to extended substance or body. [Intellectual] perception, volition, and all the modes both of perceiving and of willing are to be referred to thinking substance; while to extended substance belong size (that is extension in length, breadth and depth), shape, motion, position, divisibility of component parts and the like. But we also experience within ourselves certain other things which *must not be referred either to the mind alone or to the body alone*. These arise … from the close and intimate union of our mind with the body. This list includes, first, appetites like hunger and thirst; secondly, the emotions or passions of the mind which do not consist of thought alone, such as the emotions of anger, joy, sadness and love; and finally all the sensations such as those of pain, pleasure, light, colours, sounds, smells, tastes, heat, hardness and the other tactile qualities (AT VIIIA 23: CSM I 208–9).

Human nature and the passions

As its title implies, Descartes' last work, *Les passions de l'âme*, completed just before his ill-fated visit to Sweden in 1649, was a detailed study of the passions, modalities of experience that are unique to the mind–body union, and which testify to the fact that we are not pure *res cogitantes* or 'thinking things', but are *humans*, whose day-to-day lives are intimately bound up with bodily states and events. One can, presumably, imagine beings whose lives operated on a purely intellectual level, who calmly contemplated those propositions that rational analysis reveals to be true, and calmly pursued those goals that are rationally perceived to be beneficial. Such a life would perhaps be 'superior' to ours, in the sense of being free from the tensions and turmoil that often arise from the bodily side to our nature; but it would also be strangely 'colourless' in comparison with the vivid interplay of emotion and feeling that characterizes human existence.

Some of these contrasts were explored by Descartes in a letter written to the French ambassador to Sweden, who had asked him, on behalf of Queen Christina, to explain his views on the subject of love:

> In answer to your question I make a distinction between the love which is purely intellectual or rational, and the love which is a passion. The first, in my view, consists

simply in the fact that when our soul perceives some present or absent good, which it judges to be fitting for itself, it joins itself to it willingly ...

But when our soul is joined to the body, this rational love is commonly accompanied by the other kind of love, which can be called sensual or sensuous. This ... is nothing but a confused thought aroused in the soul by some motion of the nerves ... Just as in thirst the sensation of the dryness of the throat is a confused thought which disposes the soul to desire to drink, but is not identical with that desire, so in love a mysterious heat is felt around the heart, and a great abundance of blood in the lungs which makes us open our arms as if to embrace something, and this inclines the soul willingly to join to itself the object presented to it. There is no reason to be surprised that certain motions of the heart should be naturally connected in this way with certain thoughts, which they in no way resemble. The soul's natural capacity for union with a body brings with it the possibility of an association between each of its thoughts and certain motions or conditions of this body, so that when the same conditions recur in the body, they induce the soul to have the same thought ... (AT IV 601–4: CSMK 306–7).

The idea of psycho-physical *associations* which Descartes alludes to here is the key to his view of what it is like to be a human being. Some of the associations are 'natural', or, as he sometimes says, 'divinely ordained', such as the sensation of thirst which we feel when the throat is dry. We might now say that these are genetically programmed into

52

the species, as a result of their obvious survival value in the struggle for existence; what Descartes says, in pre-Darwinian mode, is that

> any given movement occurring in the part of the brain that immediately affects the mind produces just one corresponding sensation; and hence the best system that could be devised is that it should produce the one sensation which of all possible sensations is most especially and most frequently conducive to the preservation of the healthy man. And experience shows that the sensations which nature has given us are all of this kind; and so there is absolutely nothing to be found in them that does not bear witness to the power and goodness of God (AT VII 87: CSM II 60).

Other associations are generated environmentally, as a result of repeated patterns of stimulus and response. Descartes here uses the example of animal training (strikingly anticipating the much later Pavlovian theory of conditioned reflexes):

> I reckon that if you whipped a dog five or six times to the sound of a violin, it would begin to howl and run away as soon as it heard that music again (letter to Mersenne of 18 March 1630, AT I 134: CSMK 20).

And, finally, there are beneficial associations that we can decide to set up not in animals but in ourselves; we can, in short, 'reprogram' the operation of the passions to enable us to lead a better and more fulfilled life:

> When a dog sees a partridge it is naturally disposed to

53

run towards it; and when it hears a gun fired, the noise naturally impels it to run away. Nevertheless, setters are commonly trained so that the sight of partridge makes them stop, and the noise they hear afterwards, when someone fires at the bird, makes them run towards it. These things are worth noting in order to encourage each of us to make a point of controlling our passions. For since we are able, with a little effort, to change the movements of the brain in animals devoid of reason, it is evident that we can do so still more effectively in the case of human beings. Even those who have the weakest souls could acquire absolute mastery over all their passions, if we employed sufficient ingenuity in training and guiding them. (*Passions of the Soul*, art. 50, AT XI 370: CSM I 348).

The 'substantial union' of soul and body that constitutes a human being requires, for its survival and wellbeing, not just intellect and volition, but the whole range of sensory and affective states. All sensory states, as we have seen, are attributable to us not *qua* pure 'thinking things', but *qua* embodied creatures – human beings. And it is clear that many of the psycho-physical correlations involved are crucial for our survival, both as individuals and as a species: that we feel a characteristic kind of discomfort when the stomach is empty and the blood sugar is low has obvious survival value in impelling us to eat (and thus relieving the feeling of hunger); that I feel pain when I tread on a thorn has evident utility in encouraging me to avoid such noxious stimuli in future. The susceptibility of the passions to reprogramming, moreover, opens the possibility of our using the mind–body associations to our own advantage; unlike the animals, who are 'lumbered' with genetically and environmentally determined patterns of response, the human being is in the unique position of being able to put the associative patterns to the service of a rationally planned vision of the good life.

Descartes' conclusion is that the passions that arise from our bodily inheritance are to be embraced, since their operation, in general, is intimately related to our human welfare. This is not to say that they are always and uncontroversially good. Because of the relatively rigid way innate physiological mechanisms and environmentally conditioned responses operate, we may become locked into behaviour that leads to distress, misery or harm. The dropsical man, to use one of Descartes' instances, feels a strong desire to drink, even when fluid is the last thing his health requires (Sixth Meditation, AT VII 89: CSM II 61); or, to take an intriguing example from Descartes' own life, the philosopher found himself in the grip of an unfortunate attraction to all cross-eyed women, just because as a boy he had fallen in love with a girl with a squint (letter to Chanut of 6 June 1647, AT V 57: CSMK 323). But the appropriate way to cope with such irrational impulses is, for Descartes, not to retreat to an austere intellectualism, nor to suppress the passions, but rather to use the resources of science and experience to try to understand what has caused things to go wrong, and then to attempt to reprogram our responses so that the direction in which we are led by the passions corresponds to what our reason perceives as the best option:

Often passion makes us believe certain things to be much better and more desirable than they are; then, when we have taken much trouble to acquire them, and in the process lost the chance of possessing other more genuine goods, possession of them brings home to us their defects; and thence arise dissatisfaction, regret and remorse. And so the true function of reason is to examine the just value of all the goods whose acquisition seems to depend in some way on our conduct, so that we never fail to devote all our efforts to trying to secure those which are in fact the more desirable ...

Often however the passions ... represent the goods to which they tend with greater splendour than they deserve, and they make us imagine pleasures to be much greater before we possess them than our subsequent experiences show them to be ... But the true function of reason in the conduct of life is to examine and consider without passion the value of all the perfections, both of the body and of the soul, which can be acquired by our conduct, so that since we are commonly obliged to deprive ourselves of some goods in order to acquire others, we shall always choose the better (letter to Elizabeth of 1 September 1645, AT IV 284–5, 286–7: CSMK 264–5).

Despite the alienation from the body which Cartesian dualism often seems to threaten, Descartes' final vision of the human condition is characterized by an engaging realism and, ultimately, by a humane optimism. Strange hybrid creatures compounded of pure mind and mechanical body, we nonetheless enjoy, at the level of our ordinary daily experience, a whole range of sensory and emotional responses whose operation, in the first place, is designed to conduce in general to human fulfilment, and which, in the second place, we have the power to modify and reprogram to our own advantage. As Descartes resoundingly declared to a correspondent in 1648:

> The philosophy I cultivate is not so savage or grim as to outlaw the operation of the passions; on the contrary, it is here, in my view, that the entire sweetness and joy of life is to be found (letter to Silhon of March or April 1648: AT V 135).

Of course, the road ahead, as Descartes sometimes acknowledged, will often be a difficult one: the strength of the passions can lead us to put them to bad use, and the way things work out is, in any case, influenced by the external dimension of fortune, over which we have no control. There are no guarantees. But the nobility of the Cartesian vision of the human condition lies in its clear-eyed acceptance of this, and of the inherent frailty, yet possibility of joy, that arises from the inescapably corporeal side to our humanity:

> The pleasures common to soul and body depend entirely on the passions, so that persons whom the passions can move most deeply are capable of enjoying the sweetest pleasures of this life. It is true that they may also experience the most bitterness when they do not know how to put these passions to good use, and when fortune works against them. But the chief use of wisdom lies in teaching us to be masters of our passions and to

control them with such skill that the evils which they cause are quite bearable, and even become a source of joy (*Passions of the Soul*, art. 212, AT XI 488: CSM I 404).